M000114199

This Journal Belongs To

Jarslie Publishing – jarlsie.com

Made in United States
North Haven, CT
09 October 2022

25213612R00075